On Top Of The Wardrobe
A Poetry Hotchpotch

On Top Of The Wardrobe
is a chaotic compilation of poetry and artwork

by Patricia Little

Copyright 2021

All rights reserved. No part of this publication may be reproduced, stored in a retrieval system or transmitted in any form or by any means, electronic, mechanical, photocopy, recording or otherwise, without prior written consent of the copyright owner. Nor can it be circulated in any form of binding or cover other than that in which it is published and without similar condition including this condition being imposed on a subsequent purchaser.

The right of Patricia Little to be identified as the author of this work has been asserted in accordance with the Copyright Designs and Patents Act 1988.

A copy of this book is deposited with the British Library

On Top Of The Wardrobe

978-1-8382744-8-1

Patricia Little

Published By: -

i2i Publishing. Manchester.

www.i2ipublishing.co.uk

Tables of Contents

Don't Trust a Policeman 1

Days of Steam 3

Childhood Bliss 4

The Map Worm 5

Poor Henry 7

Speak Up 10

A Summer Sky 11

Hang Up 13

Think of Me 14

Yesterdays and Tomorrows 15

A Page in a Book 16

Come Waltz With Me 17

Teething Troubles 18

Divine Intervention 19

The Sonnet of Double Cream 21

Shakespeare's Haemorrhoids 22

Welcome to my Brain 23

The Dusts of Time 24

All The Fun of The Fair 25

Feet 27

When We Were Young 29

Nature's Gems 31

My Captured Heart	33
The Poets Waltz	34
Ode to a Cheese Grater	35
Sepia Moments	36
She Loves Me, She Loves Me Not	37
The Housewife's Lament	38
The Thing of Dreams	39
Fidget	40
Cure All	41
Saturday Night 1959	43
Our Loo	45
Bin Slave	46
Days	47
The Gift	48
Do I Come Here Often?	49
If	50
Getting Younger	51
Waiting	53
Without Our Dreams	54
Smile Please	55
The Worried Doughnut	56
Halcyon	57
Tears of Snow	58
Endless	59
Spring	60

Old Poetry Inspires	61
Take My Hand	62
Aisle 3	63
Local History	65
Another Day	67
A Breath in Time	68
Graveyard Hill	69
The Merry - Go - Round	70
Seasons	71
The Rose	72
Grandma's Garden	73
The Fairy's Harp	75
Another Autumn	76
Merrion's Wood	77
The Bugle Boy	79
How Shall I Go?	80
The Tortoise	81
I Love My Shoes	83
The Wrong Nose	84
On Top of The Wardrobe	85
Roller Skating Granny	87
Multi Tasking	89
The Brolly With Angst	91
Grapevine	93
Too Tall For The Box	95

The Dreaded Mobile Phone 97

The Tale of Thomas McBraie 99

The Driggly 101

Looking For Santa 103

My Diet Diary 105

My Birthday Surprise 107

Out To Graze 109

Christmas Day In The Workhouse 111

Grandad's Been At The Bottle 113

Choose Cheese 114

Exercise 115

The Grass is Always Greener 116

Fried or Boiled 117

Epitaph 118

———

About the Author 119

Don't Trust A Policeman

While looking for petrol,
my needle was low,
a cop pulled me over,
for driving too slow.

He said 'I must stop you,
but don't worry miss.
I just have to ask you,
to blow into this.'

Then out from his pocket,
he fetched a balloon.
'It's our Sergeant's birthday
I must be there quite soon.

I've been chasing burglars,
and that kind of stuff.
Will you blow my balloon up?
I'm all out of puff.

If you fancy a party,
I'll take you there too.'
I blew his balloon up.
What else could I do?

But then he just left me.
Drove off in the night.
The last thing I saw dear,
was a flash of blue light.

Now you've heard my story.
It's very sad stuff,
when a cop takes advantage
of a girl with more puff.

Let this be a lesson
to learn pretty soon.
Just don't trust a policeman,
if he's got a balloon.

Days of Steam

*When was that final day, when dreams
were wrapped in sulphured smoke;
as Jack stoked up the boiler
with his final spade of coke?
I never took a moment,
never kissed that age goodbye.
I just remember watching,
as my dreams curled to the sky.
I wish I could step back in time;
revisit just to see, those hidden
faces glimpsed through steam,
hands waving back at me;
a little girl in buttoned boots
who watched the trains pass by.
Which day was that? How many
dreams have vanished in the sky?
I need to grasp that moment
but my memory slips away.
I want to be that girl again and
make that moment stay.
But time has crept unnoticed;
it's too late we can't go back
to the happy days of childhood,
spent near that railway track.*

Childhood Bliss

Lazy days, crazy days,
lying in the sun days.
Chasing games, hiding games.
Play pretend and nicknames.
Keepsake treasures,
childhood pleasures.
Sack races, secret places.
Climbing trees with grubby faces.

Late to bed and early rises.
Grandpa's visit; nice surprises.
Grandma's kiss, childhood bliss.
Scrapbook snips, seaside trips.
Orange peel and apple pips.
Candy-floss; sticky hands.
Stripy deck-chairs, village bands.
Day's sublime; summertime.

The Map-Worm

*There's a bookshop down the street,
where the bookworms tend to meet;
each one of them is on a similar mission.
Where each is searching through,
piles of books; both old and new,
always hoping that they'll find that first edition.*

*There's a box of cartographic,
full of dust from passing traffic;
each map has extra creases to it's face.
No longer being needed,
for the days have long receded,
when explorers carried them from place to place.*

*Old fingerprints still showing,
the way that they'd be going;
past viewpoints that might lead to hidden glen.
Each picnic place we find,
by the tea-stain left behind,
as we follow in the footsteps of these men.*

Up mountains maps have hiked,
in panniers they have biked.
In any weather; sunshine, snow or rain.
For even soaking wet,
these maps never failed to get,
intrepid travellers there and back again.

But for all the tales it's told;
every tear and every fold,
it's use today is for the likes of me.
For I have a fascination
for each by-way, each plantation;
a work of art whose beauty I still see.

Though it's sad I know I must,
leave it there to gather dust.
Redundant now, it's way too out of date.
For we see no motorways,
criss-crossing quiet days.
A GPS is now the travellers mate.

Poor Henry

Henry loved his sticky toffee,
treacle pudding, cream banoffee.
Chocolate running down his chin;
he'd grab still more and cram it in.
His cheeks would bulge with so much food;
to say "no thanks" he thought was rude.

His parents seemed to think him thin;
to offer fruit they thought a sin.
'Come on now son, eat up your cake,
a fine young man, one day you'll make.'
So with pork pies he'd saved for later
Henry took the elevator.

Stepping on, feet side by side,
young Henry thought he'd take a ride.
The elevator didn't budge,
the folks behind gave him a nudge.
'You'll have to walk' the people shouted.
'You're far too fat.' Poor Henry pouted.

Alas it didn't stop him eating;
bad habits Henry kept repeating.
One day when going into church,
young Henry felt his tummy lurch.

Just as the choir 'Rejoicing' sang,
poor Henry's tummy went off bang

and as they reached the highest note,
they recognised poor Henry's coat.
Floating down from realms above;
as if from angels, sent with love.
'It's still like new' said Henry's Dad,
'we'll keep it for our other lad,'

The Vicar looked in sad despair
at bits of Henry everywhere,
feeling quite exasperated;
his Church just newly decorated.
The Verger though, was not surprised;
said 'Henry was quite over-sized.'

*So after cleaning up the pews,
the Vicar thought this chance he'd use
said; passing round collection plate,
'Let's think of Henry, and his fate.
Give generously' the Vicar calls.
'To help scrape Henry off the walls.'

And from his pulpit, loud and grim,
a lengthy sermon does begin.
'Let's pray for Henry, who it seems
ate far too many custard creams.
A habit Henry couldn't stop.
Until today – he went off pop.

God's wishes we must understand.
Dear Lord, was this what you had planned?
God's ways his servants only guess;
why did he have to leave this mess?
Though Henry was a happy soul;
we wish that he'd departed whole.

Let this sad lesson teach us all;
eating too much was his downfall
and moderation is the key
to longer lives for you and me.
God's message then with us abide
and spread like Henry: far and wide.'*

Speak Up

*She'll never make a speaker
of that we have no doubt.
She always stands there laughing,
then her false teeth fall out.
How can she go on talking
as though we're unaware,
that her words are really mumbled,
and her teeth are over there'?*

A Summer Sky

Come walk with me, let's visit once again
that special place called childhood; precious days.
Where poppies set the golden corn ablaze.
I sat and watched you make a daisy chain
and listened to a curlew's sweet refrain.
Such moments linger like a sunset's haze
to wrap me warmly in her final rays
and take me now, where memories remain.

Where did we go? We didn't say farewell.
We simply stepped into another life.
Somebody's husband; someone else's wife.
We shared a childhood 'neath a summer sky.
Yet when I hear the summer breezes sigh,
it takes me back and holds me in its spell.
How could we know back then what life had planned?
Our dreams we shared; our mountains yet to climb.
For we were young and still to reach our prime.
Our days were spent exploring new found land
We splashed through streams
our shoes held in each hand.
Such simple days; so carefree, so sublime,
still whisper down the corridors of time;
each memory a single grain of sand.

Yet life gives life and life takes life away.
What lies ahead? It's best we never know.
Some memories are sweet, while fate unkind.
The cards are dealt, but we choose how to play.
A game of chance; a simple dice to throw,
and leave life's sting forever in our mind.

What would we find if somehow we returned?
Would poppy fields still scorch the naked eye?
Would music form when hearing curlews cry?
Or would fond memories be sadly spurned?
No going back; so say the lessons learned.
Our childhood days take wings; so soon they fly.
Like hatching birds, they seek that summer sky,
and suddenly another page is turned.
Yet from my room I see those fields of gold;
a gentle sway to hypnotise the mind,
while poppies blaze their flaming shades of red.
Those childhood days within my heart I hold
and as I watch each memory unwind,
find comfort now where ageing footsteps tread.

Hang Up

Press 1 if you're a salesman with windows to install.

Press 2 if it's to tell me I've won a dream- trip to Nepal.

Press 3 if you are offering a cheaper price for gas.

Press 4 to hold forever, while I go and mow the grass.

Press 5 if you would like to hear an irritating tune, then call again in thirty twelve even that would be too soon.

Press 6 to hear this message a thousand times or more; to give you time to wonder what it was you rang me for.

Then leave it 30 seconds I suggest you count to ten. Or better still – just bugger off and please don't call again.

Think Of Me

Think of me sometimes when you're far away.
In quiet moments let thoughts reminisce.
When music taught the hands the notes to play
and found delight in each and every kiss.

The touch of softest skin and silken sheet,
as moonlight cast it's shadows etched in gold.
Remembering again where pleasures meet;
the joy exploring every secret fold.

As thoughts re-kindle special times like this,
then you will know that I remember too.
Upon your lips you'll feel my gentle kiss;
think of me then and know I think of you.

Yesterdays and Tomorrows

Don't offer me tomorrow; tomorrow may not be.
Give me today and all the days we've shared.
I'll remember every second
that you chose to spend with me;
the times I knew for certain that you cared.

Don't make me any promise
that a breeze could blow away.
Don't try to make amends; what's done is done.
Just share with me this moment,
there's no need for you to say
those words that will mean nothing once you've gone.

I don't need another sunset
that just brings a darker sky.
Nor to hear the birds announce another day.
For all our summers ended when I heard you say goodbye,
the day I stood and watched you walk away.

Don't offer me tomorrow; tomorrow may not be.
Give me today and all the days we've shared.
I'll remember every second
that you chose to spend with me;
the times I knew for certain that you cared.

A Page in a Book

You can fall in love with a smile; so they say,
or the sound of a voice or a certain look.
It takes just a second – that's what they say;
as quickly as turning a page in a book.

You're searching the crowds for that special face.
and each beat of your heart sounds more like a shout.
One minute everything seems in place,
but life as you knew it has turned inside out.

For nothing can save you; well that's what they say,
from that certain smile or that certain look.
It takes just a second – that's what they say;
as quickly as turning a page in a book.

Come Waltz With Me

Come waltz with me in morning mist,
sweet tasting rain; the perfect wine.
In forest glades where sunbeams kissed
approving nods of columbine.

We'll dance within each dewdrop pearl,
and watch each newborn leaf unfurl.
As raindrops cool my tingling spine,
let's both forget that I must leave.

Our tears soon mingling tears of rain,
to satiate the forest weave.
Come waltz with me one last refrain;
an orchestra of natures sound,

that never ends but keeps us bound,
till I return to you again.

Teething Troubles

I'm not feeling myself today and I'm really not sure why.
I can't get this old hair to curl no matter how I try.
It used to be so pretty; soft, and with a silken sheen.
It now looks like it's travelled to where the cat has been.

No worries, I can sort it; my hairdresser's coming soon
She's promised she can fit me in some time this afternoon
But still I have my worries, my life's forever fraught.
I've always been untidy so this mess I'll need to sort.

Cos I've a bigger problem, that I can't hide beneath.
I think I've accidentally got someone else's teeth.
I only took them out last night; discarded for a while.
Now I have to walk around with someone else's smile.

'Ok', you say, 'don't worry, especially if they're free.'
But every time I say a word, these teeth talk back at me.
They're really quite insulting, and you would never guess,
they had the cheek to say to me
'You're hair's a bloody mess.'

Divine Intervention

I'm not much for reading the papers;
I never believe what they say,
but sometimes they grab my attention,
like the story I saw yesterday.

I read of a weight watchers meeting
where dieters; checking their 'score'
had thought it divine intervention,
when they fell through a hole in the floor.

I bet they'd discussed expectations;
as they waited to step on the scale.
They just never guessed for a moment,
that the whole infrastructure would fail.

Imagining their consternation;
with floorboards beginning to creak,
while making a quick calculation,
of chocolates they'd eaten that week.

I see them all sat in the basement;
their leotards covered in dust,
complaining that weight watchers
conned them with recipes no one can trust.

The comments then made by their mentor;
as she stared at the mess round her feet,
'I know that we celebrate Christmas,
but blimey, how much did you eat'?

An accident 'weighting' to happen?
A problem no one had forseen?
Nowt left of the Weight Watcher's meeting,
but by God you can see where they've been!

I know that I shouldn't be laughing;
I've tried enough times in the past
to lose a few pounds after Christmas,
my efforts just don't seem to last.

My message to all of those ladies;
though your story is now widely known,
the damage you caused to that chapel,
I could probably do on my own.

The Sonnet of Double Cream

Compare me not to fresh cream bought to-day;
I am more ripened and less temperate.
My smell doth seek to take one's breath away.
My 'sell by' label's all too short a date.

Sometimes too hot, the eye of housewives shine
alas, to notice my complexion dimm'd.
No longer fair as double cream sublime.
But thy eternal summer bade, I'm binned.

By chance too late, returned to fridge, to wait
until infernal mould; so green hath grow'st.
And death shall brag, 'twas I adorned your plate.
Those pains severe, 'tis thanks to me thou ow'st.'

When thou so ill was heard to say too late,
'I think, it must be something that I ate.'

Shakespeare's Haemorrhoids

Shall I compare thee to a seat in Hell?
Thou art more ripened than the Grapes of Wrath.
I would not wish my foe this evil spell;
each step I take is pain, along life's path.

Sometimes too hot, the eye of bowel shines.
Alas, I suffer my affliction grim.
No longer fair of youth, but aged with time;
should my eternal piles, require a trim?

This very thought I cannot contemplate.
Each day in still more numbers; how thou grow'st.
And Death shall brag 'for me thou cannot wait;
this pain severe, 'tis thanks to piles thou ow'st.'

Oh haemorrhoids, my very soul doth crown
and pains me even more, when sitting down.

Welcome to my Brain

Welcome to my brain,
though the light has long gone out.
You might have to bring a torch,
to find your way about.

Now over in this corner
my secrets are all kept.
I really can't show those to you,
please by-pass with respect.

And here we have my poems.
Take a peek, I'd like you to.
Though you won't find an erotic one,
and nothing's ever blue.

Your visit won't take very long.
My brain is very small.
In fact I think you'll be hard pushed,
to find anything at all.

The Dusts of Time

Life's highways etched like each forgotten place;
the ups and downs now contours on her brow.
The gentle curves fond memories still chase,
through many crossroads long forgotten now.

Each worried line must have a tale to tell;
a fascinating life of times long gone.
While in the past her thoughts will often dwell,
along the dusty road she'll carry on.

Her gentle face still smiles a youthful smile,
as though she knows what waits around the bend.
Maybe a yard, or still another mile,
she knows that soon she'll find her journey's end.

Proud then, her face will wear the dusts of time.
The rest of us still have those hills to climb.

All The Fun of The Fair

Let's go on The Waltzers Mary.
Remember all the fun we had;
when that lad would spin us round
till we couldn't feel the ground,
then he got a thumping from your Dad?

Let's go on The Ghost Train Walter.
Remember how we used to scream;
and that chap climbed on board
just to scare your sister Maud,
till she splattered him with her ice cream?

Let's go on The Big Wheel Mary.
The view's so lovely from the top.
We used to sit there holding hands
looking out across the sands,
just wishing that the rain would stop.

Let's go on The Dodgems Walter,
but you'll be the one that has to drive.
I'm sure they'll let us on,
they wont know I'm eighty one
and they'll never guess you're ninety five.

Feet

I don't want a facelift to look young again.
I don't want to diet to be a size ten.
I don't want a sex change to call myself Ken.
I just want comf'table feet.

I don't want an implant for a 44A
I don't want a lipo to suck fat away.
I don't want my colon flushed out in a tray.
I just want comf'table feet.

I don't want to laser the hair on my chin.
I don't want a botoxed, permanent grin.
I don't want a belly that's nipped and tucked in.
I just want comf'table feet.

I don't want hypnosis; I don't smoke or drink.
I don't want my skin peeled and find I can't blink.
I don't want advice from a personal shrink.
I just want comf'table feet.

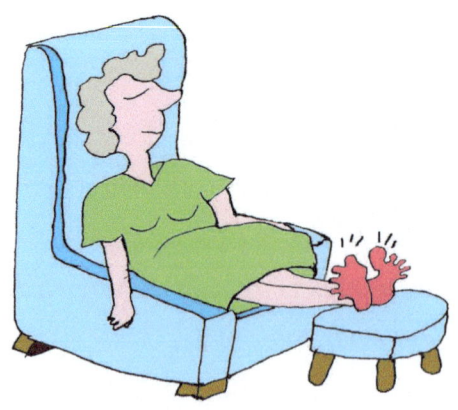

I don't want a massage while covered in clay.
I don't want a smoothie of seaweed each day.
I don't want to hear what the experts might say.
I just want comf'table feet.

Feet with new arches; feet that can dance.
Feet that can ramble from here to France.
Feet that don't rest on a stool every chance.
I just want comf'table feet.

When We Were Young

Come dance with me, my darling dear;
just like when we were young.
I want once more, to hold you near,
let's play our favorite song.
I fell in love, my darling dear,
when you were seventeen.
Your lovely eyes, so crystal clear;
one blue and t'other green.

That night with you my darling dear,
we danced to Kenny Ball.
I'm four foot three; quite small I fear
and you were eight feet tall.
But when you smiled, my darling dear,
you loved me; I could tell.
Your pretty smile, from ear to ear;
went round the back as well.

I took your hand, my darling dear,
I have it to this day. For it was false,
it would appear; but I loved you anyway.
And then you danced, my darling dear
with my mate, handsome Jack.
Your wooden leg made him feel queer,
so he quickly brought you back.

That wooden leg, my darling dear,
had termites; what a chore.
So I fitted casters at the rear,
and I wheeled you round the floor.
We danced so well, my darling dear,
my head tucked 'neath your chest.
I couldn't see which way to steer
so you whispered 'east' then 'west'

Do you remember, darling dear;
we won the 'lucky spot'?
The prize they gave, eight pints of beer.
To cheers, you drank the lot.
Oh Mildred love, my darling dear
my eyes are growing dimmer.
Let's dance again, come hold me near;
this time, without your zimmer.

Nature's Gems

*Oh give me gems of nature
that only you can bring;
the lark's song in the morning
and the early buds of Spring.*

*Show me how your palette
can transform our winter's scene;
your paintbrush changing landscapes
where winter frosts have been.*

*I want to smell wild garlic
and aromatic pine.
Teach me how the spider spins
a complex web so fine.*

*To suddenly be tiny
so I can climb inside
the hollows of the oak tree
where sleeping creatures hide.*

Take me on a journey
where the eagles dare to fly;
to rest upon a mountain
where I can touch the sky.

Fill my ears with music
from the flowing mountain stream,
where primroses form cushions
of softest pink and cream.

Oh give me gems of nature
that only you can bring;
an early morning showcase
where diamond dew drops cling.

My Captured Heart

She asks of me to prove my love for her;
if I should seek to win this maiden's heart.
A simple task, I'll not let this deter;
although I've witnessed bolder Knights depart.

My love's so deep it probes the ocean's depth.
So bright it shines among the furthest stars.
My heart can hold within, her every breath;
to heal forever battle's wounds and scars.

But how can I be sure to reach my goal?
How can I prove to her the way I feel?
Is this enough to reach into her soul?
To get it wrong I fear my fate I'll seal.

For if my love should turn away from me,
my captured heart will never more be free.

The Poets Waltz

The sweetest words can still enrage;
it matters not how hard we strive.
Instead of flowing 'cross the page,
alas they jitterbug and jive.

Dear poets do not feel defeated;
this prayer should often be repeated:
Lord, help my verses waltz valeta
and always dance in perfect meter.

Ode to a Cheese Grater

Oh little man, my knight in armour; plated,
my humble servant always keen to please,
your use, me thinks, is often underrated;
who else could serve so delicate a cheese?
'Tis time at last to sing this grater's praise;
this soldier brave who helps to feed his troop.
There's not a house without one, I've heard said.
Essential one could say, for Bolognaise
or floating islands on an onion soup.
His efforts may be thick or finely shred.

Today you begged me take you from the drawer;
seducing me again with toothy grin.
Your rugged touch you offered me once more,
then gratingly relieved me of my skin.
Perhaps my love for you was overrated;
so shamed was I, as I was playing host,
and guests began to leave and say goodnight.
In future I'll buy cheese that's ready grated.
Since finding fingernails upon their toast,
I'm left alone with just my trusted Knight.

Sepia Moments

*Lost faces staring back with sepia skin
enquire 'Who's this, who steps inside our past.
Who takes this album from it's shelf at last
and peeks with probing eyes at what's within.*

*Who hopes to find some secret, hidden sin'?
An insight to a time that vanished fast.
When was it that the family die was cast;
determining who'd fail and who would win?*

*Each page I turn reveals a moment gone;
a wedding here, a birth and there – a death.
No smiling face, straight backs on each, I see.
A stoic life for each and every one.*

*A glimpse enough to take away my breath;
I close the book, for what I see is me.*

She Loves Me, She Loves Me Not

She loves me, she loves me not;
how is this going to end?
Pulling petals off a daisy;
I must be round the bend.
I'm not the sort of fella'
who pulled wings from off a fly;
perhaps I ought to tell her
and just look her in the eye.
She loves me, she loves me not;
there's still a few to go.
But is it telling me the truth,
how will I ever know?
What if she loves another,
who'll present a nice bouquet?
I doubt she'll welcome daisies;
with petals missing anyway.
She loves me, she loves me not.
My conscience asks me why,
I pull apart sweet daisies
yet I never hurt a fly?
She loves me, she loves me not.
How can love wield such power?
Oh dear, it seems – she loves me not.
I must find another flower.

The Housewife's Lament

Each day I rise to see more dust alight
where only yesterday I'd waxed and shined.
More jobs accumulating overnight.
A life of house work; I've become resigned.

If it could only vanish from my sight
I'd plan my day as only I'd designed.
No sink of dishes waiting from last night.
No hoover standing grimly to remind.

With coffee poured I'd sit by warming fire
and let the hours slip by in silent thought.
Maybe the dancing flames would then inspire
the works of wonder master poets taught.

A dream that every poet must desire;
more time to write; each precious moment sought.

The Thing of Dreams

Oh busy mind, why do you like to keep
the darkest hour for wandering around?
While other mortals choose this time to sleep,
in every worried corner you'll be found.

Still turning over thoughts from yesterday
and mulling deeds now done and words now said.
The things that can't be changed will then replay.
Oh perfect sleep; be still this busy head.

Is sleep the luxury for but the few,
who claim the perfect life that's never stressed?
No worried nights; if what they say is true.
I can't believe that they could be so blessed.

This mind is busiest at night it seems.
A night of sleep is but the thing of dreams.

Fidget

Oh calm; befuddled fidget in my mind.
Each word's insistent scramble to be first
to leave my pen, and not get left behind.
So eager then, to quench this poet's thirst.

A jigsaw puzzle mind; each piece should fit.
If only I could stop and see the whole.
To piece together slowly, bit by bit,
requires such patience and one's self control.

But when each word slides smoothly to the page,
this fidget seems to feel much more at ease.
And where each line would one time, take an age;
there now appear sweet sounds that surely please.

I ask myself who is it guides my pen;
departed souls, of much more learn-ed men'?

Cure All

Oh doctor dear I have a pain,
my heart is all a flutter.
I had to see you once again:
I've st st started now to st st stutter.

Oh patient dear you don't look well;
your heart is really beating.
Your tongue is tied and I can tell
your prescription needs repeating.

Oh doctor dear what can it be?
Have you a magic potion?
Some tablets or some herbal tea;
more of your soothing lotion?

Oh patient dear I must confess
you'll soon be feeling fine.
Pop over here, take off your dress
and place your clothes near mine.

Oh doctor dear is it bad news;
am I about to die?
Of course I'll do just as you choose
and on your couch I'll lie.

Oh patient dear you're quite alive,
but see me twice a day.
Come back again at half past five.
I'll see you straight away.

Oh doctor dear you're good to me
How can I then repay?
Just say the word and you will see
my gratitude each day.

Oh patient dear, you'll find this cure,
requires my full attention.
Let's make it three times, to be sure.
My pleasure, – do not mention.

Saturday Night 1959

The Mayfair Dance Hall, up some stairs;
cracked lino on the floor.
A married couple; sat on chairs,
charged half-a-crown at the door.
I have fond memories of Saturday night;
pink lipstick, bee-hive hair.
Pointed shoes that were much too tight.
Teddy Boys went there.
We'd hurry in and look around;
our eyes would quickly scan.
Hoping that there might be found
an unattached young man.
The pair played records; forty fives,
a Dancette on a chair.
Boys in 'brothel creepers' loved to jive.
No Fred Astaire went there.

We would dance the Mayfair bop;
the circle moving around the floor.
And when the music stopped
the boy's said 'yo bin 'ere before'?
We'd go to the loo in pairs, at break;
my friend would guard the door.
Stilettos stepping over lake
and loo paper on the floor.
The mirror on the wall was broke ;
all cracked around the edge.
My friend liked this tallish bloke
I think his name was Reg.
Names were written on the wall;
like 'I love Tommy Grere'
But one was scratched above them all
said 'Arthur Jones was 'ere'
Drainpipes were the fashion then;
long jackets with velvet collars.
A comb in their top pocket; men!
thought they looked a million dollars.
Then orange squash was carried in
at nine, upon a tray.
We'd have a drink then dance again
to Frankie Vaughan and Johnny Ray.
Saturday night at The Mayfair,
happy memories, sharing fags,
and girls with back combed hair
when we danced around our bags.

Our Loo

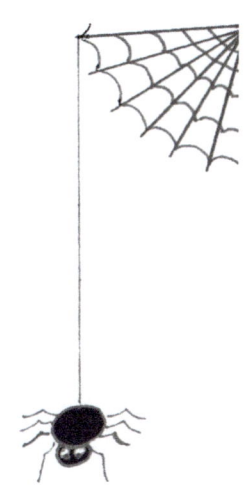

*Our loo stood down the garden
when I was a tiny child.
A cold and crumbling privy
in weeds overgrown and wild.
And when I had to visit,
till last minute I would wait;
dashing in with failing torch
I would nearly be too late!
Fixed on the wall was paper,
it was hanging on a nail;
some torn from the Daily News
and some from the Evening Mail.
Dad stayed in there for ages.
He would sit and read them all;
those little squares of paper,
while he answered nature's call.*

*I never saw the pleasure
other people seemed to find;
sitting on the wooden throne
with a freezing cold behind.
And now when I remember,
I think back about that place;
those great big creepy spiders
and the cobwebs round my face.
I wonder if it's gone now;
got bulldozed, laid to rest.
It's probably been 'listed'
as Historic Interest.*

Bin Slave

This is the tale of my old bin,
I used to put my rubbish in.
The council wasn't satisfied,
now lots of bins stand side by side.
Each has a purpose, so I'm told.
Each one instructs me what 'he'll' hold
the green, the brown, then there's the grey;
we had just black, back in the day.
I liked the black it took the lot.
Just chucked it in, didn't care a jot.
Now every tin must first be washed
and only in the grey bin – squashed.
So work for me has multiplied;
washing, squashing, then decide
which bin, which day, will it be emptied?
Never, if not 'well presented'
I'm like the planet; I need saving
from all these bins where I'm left slaving.
I know it's right I shouldn't grouse,
but my rubbish is cleaner than my house !!!

Days

How many hours are wasted every day?
How many days slip easily to years?
How many times have I been heard to say
how is it that each day just disappears?

The days when you were small flew swiftly by.
Days spent sailing, playing hockey or football.
One moment you are standing just knee high,
then suddenly one day you're six feet tall.

I'd like to think my time's been wisely spent.
Enjoying every day, I've watched you grow.
And though each day soon came, then quickly went,
how proud you make me feel, you'll never know.

Those days are where my memories began.
Which day did that young boy become a man?

The Gift

You gave me something special;
It was something just for me.
I keep it safely locked away;
I have the only key.

But when I'm feeling down
and dark clouds are all I see,
I carefully unlock your gift
and hold it close to me.

It wraps around me warmly
and it cheers me for a while.
What was it that you gave to me?
It was your lovely smile.

Do I Come Here Often?

Completely muddled in my head, I'm
Often in a spin.
Now I have to write things down.
Forgetting everythin'.
Upset at losing car keys, now my
Specs have gone amiss. I'm really getting worried, and
I'm always asking this
Old Timer's Disease, is that what's wrong?
N o of course it's not. I'm far too young!!!

If

If you can stand up straight when all around are getting canned and buying more

If just a pint or two are what you planned while others slowly slither to the floor

If you then gave a hand to those now slumped upon the ground

And smilingly refused when they all called 'another round'

If you're still feeling sober when the landlord's bell has rung

And waited as each verse of 'My Way' has been sung

If you have had the fortune to avoid a brewing fight

And quietly walked through the door and bid them all goodnight

Then I will join the rest of them and drink the cellar dry

For you my friend, will always be a better man than I.

Getting Younger

Does age really matter,
when you're old and grey?
I find it rather fun to choose
the age I'll be today.

Yesterday was wet and dull,
but I was four again.
Out I went in rubber boots,
walking in the rain.

I splashed through every puddle,
it gave some folks a smile;
but I was having fun again.
I was four just for a while.

Today the sun is shining,
I'm going to the shop.
Today I shall be seven,
I might buy a lollipop.

I see the neighbours looking;
'Eccentric' they all say.
If this is second childhood
then look out, I'm on my way.

What use comparing ailments,
discussing aching joints?
I think they're all like children
when I hear them scoring points.

Tomorrow is my birthday,
I think I shall be eight.
I might get up quite early,
or stay in bed quite late.

I may walk on the common
and if the wind is right,
I might just find I'm ten again
and try to fly a kite.

For age is just a number;
old age is what we dread.
But the only thing important
is the age inside my head.

So when folks say they're old;
no longer wish to stay alive,
I smile and say you're only young;
and me? I'm nearly five.

Waiting

*She sits before her mirror
and slowly combs her hair.
Her lipstick carefully applied;
soft rouge touched here and there.*

*She thinks she hears his footstep;
her heart quickening with joy.
At last he's coming home to her,
her darling soldier boy.*

*She knows he'll keep his promise;
he said 'darling wait for me.'
Again she looks towards the door;
she's sure she hears his key.*

*A voice says 'time for supper.'
Hands smooth her silver hair.
She says 'I hear him coming'
as they help her to her chair.*

*It's been so very long ago
she's forgotten all the pain.
In her heart she'll go on waiting.
She knows they'll meet again.*

Without Our Dreams

How silent is the night when I can't sleep,
and thoughts retrace the paths of yesteryear.
Sometimes an uphill climb forever steep;
I wonder how I got from there to here.

Why do we like to take the route that seems,
so simple when we first are starting out?
And often led by chasing fruitless dreams,
down roads that always twist and turn about.

But would we change a thing when looking back?
I doubt we'd want it any other way.
Had I the chance I'd take the same old track,
and repeat the same mistakes of yesterday.

Life has its ups and downs for us it seems.
But where would we all be without our dreams?

Smile Please

Today in the old folks home;
where Mary's days are spent,
all around the room
offering sweeties Mary went.

Everybody took one;
for it was kindly meant.
Then quickly they all spit them out
'cos it was Steredent.

Now everybody's moaning.
It goes on through the night.
Why is it such a problem?
At least their teeth are white.

Each cloud has a silver lining.
They'll find out in a while,
and we would see the benefit,
if only they would smile.

The Worried Doughnut

Will you step a little nearer,
said the doughnut to the bun.
There's a custard slice behind us,
and she seems to think it's fun,
to eat up all the cup-cakes.
She's already swallowed three.
Now she's getting closer.
I think she's after me.

She's just nibbled at the shortbread.
Don't let her see you stare.
Whoops – I don't believe it;
there goes a cream éclair.
She really is quite greedy,
and what's more, I've told her that.
You'd think she'd realise by now,
that cakes will make her fat.

Halcyon

*Memories winding through my mind
of childhood days when words were kind.
A thought, a sound, a seashell found,
sun kissed sands, young love still blind.*

*Days to cherish, so soon to fly
like seagulls to a distant sky.
Seaweed plaits; ankles bound.
Whispering grasses, curlew's cry.*

*A parasol, a smiling face
a gentle hand, a special place.
She's gone and yet she's still around;
her voice the wind; in timeless grace.*

Tears of Snow

How still it seems this silent snow can fall
as if she's whispering to sleeping birds.
While weighted branches humbly bow to all;
their twisted throats now full of frozen words.

As Winter still holds on with gripping claws;
refusing nature's call for early Spring
and daring all to open bolted doors;
her latest counterpane of snow she'll bring.

When she decides at last, it's time to go;
as sunlit fingers point accusing beam,
then Winter bids farewell, her tears of snow
drip gently down to join life's flowing stream.

Endless

As winter lingers; colours drab,
ice fingers pick at frozen scab.
Breath like a cloud, hangs in the air;
a quiet blackness everywhere.

Each winter longer than the last,
is it with age, more doubts are cast?
When summer days seem far away
and dreams are steeped in endless grey.

A single sound begs to be heard;
first early riser; bravest bird.
When will the morning sun surprise,
with primrose birth to warm our eyes?

Spring

Creatures stirring, stretching, waking.
Dragonflies, reflections making.
New born lambs, first breath taking.
Welcoming their day.

Gentle rain new growth inviting.
Dappled sunshine, woodland lighting.
Squirrels leaping; playful fighting.
Cobwebs chased away.

Foxes hungry, lurking, cunning.
Swallows swooping, feathers sunning.
Children skipping, laughing, running.
Fresh air for their play.

Natures colours bright, surround us.
Painted landscapes, all around us.
Spring's arrived, at last she's found us;
soothing frosts away.

Old Poetry Inspires

To follow in the footsteps of the Bard
and hear words seeping forth from Avon's veins,
this country's inspiration's never jarred;
the beauty Shakespeare found, she still retains.

To seek the village church revered by Gray.
The woods and groves where Milton found his muse.
And minstrels sang of where young lovers lay;
these places offered them the words to choose.

Though poetry may change with fashions new,
as poets plough their field; each one diverse,
we have to give old poets praise that's due;
for they prepared the ground with love of verse.

Old poets never die, they're still adored.
Their voices echo through the winds of time.
Their seeds were firmly set when cast abroad.
Old poetry inspires the modern rhyme.

Take My Hand

Take my hand, I promise you
I'll never let it go.
I'll take you to a special place,
where tender orchids grow.

In forest glades, on softest moss,
we'll lie; just you and I.
While nightingales will serenade
a gentle lullaby.

As moonbeams dance across your face
and dew drops kiss your eyes,
our arms entwined forever;
we'll gaze at midnight skies.

So come with me my darling
and we will never part.
For if you give your hand to me,
I'll give to you my heart.

Aisle 3

If Mr Right should come along,
will there be a flash of light,
as the sun glints on his armour,
when his horse rides into sight?

And will he sweep me off my feet
and carry me away?
No, I don't really think so.
It'll be like any day.

When he is least expected
and I'm not looking at my best,
that's when old 'fate' will intervene
and put me to the test.

I bet I'll be in Sainsburys,
just strolling down Aisle 3.
Or Morrisons or Tesco's,
they're all the same to me.

He'll be spotting OAP's
who are shopping just for one:
grabbing every bargain
before the sell by date has gone.

Will he help me gather my small change
that's scattered on the floor?
Or leave me to it, saying
that he can't bend no more!

Maybe he'll pass the cornflakes
from off the upper shelf.
Or perhaps I'll let him jump the queue
with less shopping than myself.

So if you see my Mr Right,
give him a message please:
tell him that I'm in Aisle 3,
just near the frozen peas.

Local History

*I remember local characters
when I was just a kid.
We called them tramps in those days,
well, everybody did.
Now 'Pockets', he wore several coats
and everything he found,
he stuffed in all his pockets,
as he wandered round and round.
Then there was old 'Boot Black' –
he put polish on his skin.
You couldn't see him in the dark.
You might just see his grin.
The scary one, we called him 'Chink'
We'd run if he came by.
He always had a walking stick,
'I'll hook your necks' he'd cry.
In the autumn we'd all gather
for the lights throughout the park.
Everyone would go there,
and queue till it was dark.*

*Outside the gates,
and up a pole,
there was the strangest sight.
A man squashed in a barrel.
It seems he stayed
there day and night.
He waved to us,
as he looked down,
beneath him was a sign;
'Fourteen Days'
the notice read;*

*'I've been here rain or shine.'
So where did these folk go to?
I suppose they've all passed on.
They're part of local history;
strange people; been and gone.*

Another Day

How do we choose the moment
to close the final page; to seek the peaceful calm
and douse the flames of rage?
When is the moment right, to simply walk away,
when we know that we'll be hurting
someone else along the way?

How can we see the future when our eyes are full of tears
and our brave new plans are clouded
by someone else's fears?
How do we make decisions that we know are surely right,
when everything seems simpler if we just give up the fight?
With no one left to turn to and when everything seems lost,
when do we say enough's enough;
who pays the final cost?

Which pathway do we take then; to the left or to the right
when we know that all paths lead us
to another sleepless night?
When there's no one there to listen
and the world's an empty place,
we simply start another day, with another smiling face

A Breath in Time

Life sometimes seems to blind the weary,
each crossroad shrouded; endless greying.
So hard to see the world around us;
no time to pause when heavy laden.

When looking back at life's long journey,
my mind now ponders every turning.
More time to question human weakness;
reliving every footstep taken.

For life is just the briefest moment.
Like bubbles bursting on the surface.
So cherish every second given;
take time to look and time to listen.

Live life, love life in all its glory.
We're merely a breath in time and space.

Graveyard Hill

*I wondered where I'd left my shroud
while floating low o'er Graveyard Hill.
And then I saw a happy crowd
of picnickers eager to fill
their mouths with chicken, ham and cheese,
as cake crumbs fluttered in the breeze.
'Twas then I saw that shroud of mine,
upon the ground among the fray.
My shroud now splashed with Merlot wine;
their tablecloth before them lay.
I watched amazed - in disbelief;
among this crowd, a graveyard thief!
The breeze around them danced, but they
cared not while stuffing food in glee.
A poet, dead or not, would say
'what jolly jocund company'!
I gazed – and gazed – my only thought;
the damage to my shroud they'd wrought.
Until the moment came when I
swooped down and swiftly grabbed my shroud
and floating up towards the sky,
looked down upon the scattered crowd,
with faces white and screams so shrill.
No picnics now on Graveyard Hill!.*

The Merry-Go-Round

You came into my mind again today
while watching golden horses spinning round,
with open mouths but nothing left to say;
a fairground ride, now circling free of sound.

Yet echoing those tender words you found
like music, when our heart beats seemed to rhyme.
A rhapsody so fleeting, yet profound,
that echoes in my mind from time to time.

I watch as golden horses gently climb,
ascending and descending memories.
Reflections now reminding me that I'm
still silently revolving just like these.

You came into my mind, now I'm aware,
that what I thought we had was never there.

Seasons

When Spring arrives inviting waking souls,
released at last from Winter's gripping claws.
From hibernating warmth of fireside coals
and feathered quilts and double bolted doors,

how good it feels to step outside again.
To walk in quiet woods where bluebells grow
and dappled sunshine forms a counterpane;
a gentle warming after winter's snow.

This season of new growth and fresh re-birth
lasts only for a while and then she's gone.
But long enough to know that mother earth
will breathe new life, just like she's always done.

And just as Springtime ends and bids farewell,
then Summertime arrives to cast her spell.

The Rose

A rose of multi-coloured choice
speaks many words with silent voice.
A single rose, or full bouquet
brings love that brightens any day.

So beautiful; the English rose
the lover's choice when they propose.
A posy held at maidens breast;
her wedding day with roses blessed.

Offered too in friendship's gift
when spirits need an extra lift.
Always in that final wreath
to say we're sharing in your grief.

Of all the roses loved by all;
in country lanes from spring 'til fall
my choice, if asked, would always be
the briar rose, just rambling free.

Grandma's Garden

I want to visit one last time
a place of long ago,
where honeysuckle fills the air
and wild violas grow.

Where Grandma grew her sunflowers;
so tall compared to me.
Where lavender swayed gently
to coax the bumble bee.

We'd sit beneath the apple tree
and watch the sun go down.
While butterflies stretched out
their wings on purple thistle down.

Her garden was a magic place
with colours changing hue.
Tall hollyhocks, delphiniums
in shades of deepest blue.

I wonder if it's still the same,
if Grandma's waiting there.
I wonder if she'll call my name;
place flowers in my hair.

So come with me my little one
and hold me by the hand.
I'll take you to a garden
that my dearest Grandma planned.

We'll sit beneath the apple tree,
you'll smell the perfumed air
and I will make a daisy chain
for your pretty golden hair.

The Fairy's Harp

Come with me to the woods again,
in April sun and gentle rain.
Let's listen to that soft refrain.
The fairy's harp you'll hear.
The rippling brook, its music flows.
The soughing leaves, soft tempo knows,
and as their joined crescendo grows,
The fairy's harp plays near.
There's magic music all around.
In all the trees, and o'r the ground.
An orchestra of nature's sound.
The fairy's harp rings clear.
Let's stay until the silver moon,
is beckoned by the fairy's tune.
A night of magic, gone too soon
as dewdrops now appear.
But we can go there any day.
Just close your eyes, let memories stray.
In dreams you'll gently float away.
The fairy's harp you'll hear.

Another Autumn

Another Summer passes, Autumn too.
The leaves seem anxious now to leave the tree.
Their game of chase I watch with thoughts of you;
they whisper to each other 'wait for me.'

These words you said to me so long ago,
re-kindle as each Autumn passes by.
Each year I've walked this path although I know,
that when you said farewell you meant goodbye.

The leaves like swirling thoughts around my head,
form pictures in my mind to bring you near.
One leaf remaining now, hangs by a thread.
One hope, that there's a chance I'll find you here.

Another Autumn dances round each tree.
Her leaves are whispering softly 'wait for me.'

Merrion's Wood

I love to walk in Merrion's Wood,
such peaceful thoughts it brings.
Where dappled sunshine filters
through, and nesting birdlife sings.

Such inspiration all around,
with colours changing hue.
Dragonflies like fairies, dip
towards the morning dew.

It's here imagination soars,
like swallows flying high.
While nature paints her picture,
'gainst a water colour sky.

I step with care through bluebells.
Drifts of purple, shades of blue.
Pink purslane and wild pansies.
There's the gentle primrose too.

Each walk I take inspires me,
she enfolds me in her arms.
Enthralled by all her beauty,
I'm seduced by nature's charms.

She poses in her glory.
Her accomplishments I see.
It's as though she's saying to us,
'here's my palette, please paint me.'

I breathe in all these colours.
Capture moments in my mind.
I hope that when I'm painting,
this memory will re-wind.

If my efforts then on canvas,
could be but half as good,
as the splendours that surround me,
on my walk in Merrion's Wood.

The Bugle Boy

Who will remember the bugle boy?
Who knows the place where he fell?
Where he lay alone on the cold wet ground
while death played it's dreadful knell.

Who would know of his final thoughts?
Who was there at his final breath?
Who will have held the young boy's hand
as he faced his lonely death?

His bones still lie on a foreign field
far from the stone that lists those lost.
Who reads the names of those gallant men?
Who was left counting the cost?

The blood still stains the silent soil
that covered the young boy's face
and a bugle plays through the winds of time
where poppies now mark the place.

Who will remember the bugle boy;
who lived and died too soon?
Who grieved the loss of the bugle boy?
Who played his final tune?

How Shall I Go?

How shall I go, when I am asked to leave?
When death decides it's time to bid farewell,
shall I go smiling, saying do not grieve?
Will I be pleased? If only truth could tell.

What man can say? Of all those gone before
no one returned; no chance to change one's mind.
Maybe it's true, when called through heaven's door
a better place than here, is what I'll find.

Is it enough to claim I've done my best?
How are we judged; by points marked out of ten?
What makes one man stand out above the rest?
Will I be told – go – do it all again?

All I can say; when life gives up the fight,
what's done is done - I hope I did it right.

The Tortoise

It was a day I shall remember;
one no-one would forget.
My young son, then aged seven,
said he'd like a little pet.
'So what pet would you like son'?
'A tortoise' he would shout.
So off we went to buy one.
And the man then picked one out.
Jack couldn't wait to get it home.
He put it on the lawn.
But it never seemed to move about.
t just stayed put till dawn.
He'd given it some clover.
I'd bought a lettuce too.
I could see we had a problem.
So now what could we do?
The tortoise wasn't living.
To the shop, we all marched in.
Our Jack was standing crying.
The man said 'What's up with him'?
I said 'you've sold a dead one.
We've had to bring it back.
That's an awful thing to happen,
upsetting our son Jack.'

The man then took the tortoise
and tested every joint.
In and out he pulled his legs.
He tried hard to prove a point.
But the man had to admit it
the tortoise, it was dead.
'I don't know how that happened,
choose another one he said.'
And there, nearby the counter,
I could see were four or five.
The man picked up the smallest.
Saying 'look this ones alive.'
He pulled it's little legs out.
Just like he'd done before.
I said 'Don't do that to him'
I couldn't take much more.
Jack went up to the counter.
The biggest one he found.
The man sucked air between his teeth.
'That one's another pound.'
I said 'you must be joking,
all those miles that we've just done.
Carrying round a tortoise
that's long been dead and gone'?
He said 'Ok just take it.'
Jack's face was full of smiles.
His dad was not so happy.
We'd just done forty miles.

I Love My Shoes

I love my shoes so dearly,
and both with equal share.
I love the left and I love the right.
Well, I only wear one pair.
Don't offer your condolence.
Don't send money, – I'm ok.
I used to wear nice pointy shoes,
till my arches fell one day.
Why is it that all pretty shoes
are made for feet so thin?
They don't allow for bunions,
you just can't squeeze them in.
And those gorgeous little ankle straps,
now that's what really rankles.
How am I supposed to fasten them,
with my poor swollen ankles?
So I just dream of lovely shoes.
But my worry now can stop.
'Cos only yesterday I've found,
this pretty, jewelled flip-flop.

The Wrong Nose

On the other side of Mars,
where no-one's ever been,
the men have bright red noses
and the ladies all have green.
On the other side of Mars,
the part that's out of sight,
their noses can confuse you,
cos they look like traffic lights.

On the other side of Mars,
the bit that's not in view,
take care at all the cross-roads,
if their noses flash at you.
On the other side of Mars,
they'll soon slap you in the nick,
if you're not careful with your driving
and the wrong nose you might pick.

On Top Of The Wardrobe

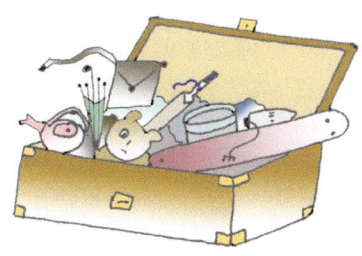

*On top of the wardrobe,
all covered in dust,
there lies an old suitcase,
full of things that are bust.*

*There's mom's old umbrella,
that blew inside out.
Dad says he can fix it,
but this we all doubt.*

*There's Granny's old teapot,
something's wrong with the spout.
Don't waste your Darjeeling,
'cos nothing comes out.*

*There's Johnny's old skateboard.
It's just lying there.
The wheels are all missing,
so it don't go nowhere.*

*Why keep all this rubbish
that's no flipping good?
'Cos dad says he'll sort it.
We just wish he would.*

*So if something needs mending,
don't give it to him.
He'll promise to fix it,
but that's just a whim.*

*It ends up on the wardrobe
all covered in dust,
inside an old suitcase,
full of things that are bust.*

Roller Skating Granny

I love my next door neighbours.
They're a wonderful old pair.
And though they're getting on in years.
Their sense of fun's still there.

The trouble is they're out late;
on the yard with all their friends.
Although it's nearly midnight,
the party never ends.

I try to read my book in bed,
but I really cannot win.
Old Albert's on the Guinness.
and Mabel's on the gin.

What's going up the entry now?
This noise it just won't do.
A roller skating granny!!
Believe me, – it's all true.

Oh let them have their fun then.
'Their getting old' I think.
But I'm really being generous,
and I just can't sleep a wink.

But listen…it's all quiet.
They've stopped for goodness sake.
I bet they're all now fast asleep,
and me – I'm wide awake.

Multi Tasking

What a day, I've often said,
when chaos reigns inside my head.
Multi-tasking is an art;
prioritise – that's where I'll start.

Late for school was first commotion;
reaching for my headache potion.
Homework missing and shoe has gone.
'Well find it dear, or wear just one.'

Washing's done – it's all turned pink;
it's those red football socks I think.
Boil it 'til it's white as snow.
T-shirt's shrunk - another blow.

Washing's out – the day looks fine;
fetch it in for umpteenth time.
Sheet was dragging on the floor;
in it goes to wash once more.

Tried to open back door quick.
Damn, too late; the dog's been sick.
Looks like he's chewed this mornings post.
What's that smell? it's burning toast.

Neighbour keeps me at the door;
gossip that I've heard before.
On and on she likes to drone.
'Have to go, I hear the phone.'

'You've won a kitchen' young man cries.
Just bugger off and stick your prize.'
Need a drink to soothe my head,
Oh God, I wish I'd stayed in bed.

The Brolly With Angst

I'm the brolly, 'she' forgot.
You know, the usual tale.
Carried here and carried there,
in case of rain or hail.

Yesterday was just the same;
taken for a ride.
Then every time the sun came out,
my nuisance 'she' would chide.

I'm just not appreciated.
I'm the one that they forget.
The only time they yearn for me,
is when they're soaking wet.

They were having tea and cream cakes,
while I lie here on the floor.
Then they see that flipping sunshine
and they're heading out the door.

So once again I'm cast aside;
kicked underneath a chair.
I know I'm in a tea-shop,
but I've no idea of where.

I'm hoping now, that some old dear,
will have a lucky find.
Then I'll be treated kindly,
no longer left behind.

I know that I'm just dreaming;
feeling sorry for my self.
But next time that it is raining,
I'll be missing from the shelf.

And boy, won't she be sorry.
From the hairdresser she'll trot,
and when it's hissing down she'll yearn,
for the brolly she forgot.

Grapevine

*It's lucky that you've caught me
for I've just arrived you see.
Not long got back from dancing,
now I need a cup of tea.
Today was my first lesson;
nothing posh, no pas de-deux.
Though I'm really rather nimble
and my waltz can cause a stir.
But we didn't need a partner,
or so I understood.
At just two pounds a session,
well, it sounded rather good.
They all appeared quite casual;
not dressed up to the nines
The room a haze of denim blue,
I watched them dance in lines.
'Ok' I thought, 'I'll join them'
and I tagged on to a row ;
'pretend that I'm an expert
and I'll follow where they go.'
My thumbs tucked into trousers;
I tried to seem real cool.*

The teacher shouted 'grape vine'
that's when I looked a fool.
'Left, rock forward, shuffle, turn'
I turned but found them gone,
For they'd all danced off one way,
and me – I'd carried on.
I pulled myself together,
'no one's looking – no one cares'
I hoped they hadn't noticed
I was in amongst the chairs.
I quickly re-assembled,
shuffled in and joined the throng;
I started off ok again,
but soon was going wrong.
The lady that I'd followed
made a turn and changed her place.
One moment I was doing well,
then we were face to face.
Another flipping 'grapevine'
now they do it in reverse.
I thought I was improving,
but instead I'm getting worse.
As I make a swift departure
I hear 'grapevine' one more time,
and their sequined denim shimmers
as they heel toe in a line.

Too Tall For The Box

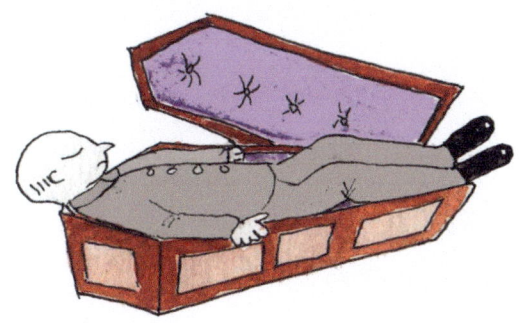

When Walter sadly passed away
the coffins seemed so small.
The Funeral Director said
'Poor Walter's far too tall.'

They tucked his arms in sideways.
They also bent him double.
But even though they pushed and pulled,
Walter still caused trouble.

'We'll never get him in this box,
the problem needs more thought.'
He considered their suggestions,
then outside help was sought.

Now, Walt had fitted carpets.
For years this was his job.
Then someone had a bright idea,
'Let's ask Walt's partner Bob.'

So the Funeral Director said
'I'll give that chap a call.'
Bob said 'The answer's easy.
Just lay him wall to wall.'

The Dreaded Mobile Phone

*Am I the only person
that hates the mobile phone?
Surely all your calls can wait
until you're back at home.*

*Can't you see you look so silly
with that thing stuck round your ear?
Talking to yourself,
like some old demented dear.*

*I'm enjoying window shopping,
but you're standing next to me.
Discussing where you're going
and what you fancy for your tea.*

*Now it's happening in Tesco's
I try ignoring what's being said;
that they haven't any lamb chops
so will a chicken do instead?*

I'm just not very bothered
what you'll wear on Friday night,
or who's going out with who
and that your friend's met Mr Right.

But for my Christmas present
I received the latest phone.
They said 'mom, you're going to need it.
You should have one of your own'.

So I said 'ok I'll take it
when I next go out alone'.
But for days nobody rang me.
Not a peep came from my phone.

So I told them 'This phone's useless,'
as I'm hanging up my coat.
And they all fell over laughing.
'Mom – That's the new CD remote.'

The Tale of Thomas McBraie

I'll tell of the maidens of Plymouth,
and a sailor named Thomas McBraie
Who courted a lass in every port
then left 'em in t' family way.

Our Tom had an extra long spy-glass
and could spot a lass even from ship.
And way before ship was in t' harbour,
was admiring the sway of her hip.

The girls they all fell for his ardour;
Tom 'specially liked maidens of class.
But the thing the girls mostly admired,
was Thomas's long spying glass.

Now whenever the girls mentioned marriage,
our Thomas would give them the slip
and quickly he'd pick up his spy-glass,
and promptly head back to his ship.

*One day Tom was walking in t' harbour
where he'd had far too many a dram;
he soon was surrounded by maidens,
and each of them pushing a pram.*

*'Now what'll 'e do then'? said Alice;
as Tom tried to run for his life.
But Thomas was still seeing double,
and what Tom didn't want was a wife.*

*But the lassies had different ideas
and pinning him down on the grass;
they soon tarred and feathered his ardour,
and put pay to his long spying glass.*

The Driggly

Oh Sire, there is a Driggly in yon moat,
and he's eating all thy stummly poppin fricks.
And though yon Driggly wears a chuddy scote,
yon peasants keep on poking it with sticks.

Shall I fetch the grindley dib from the well;
to frip it Sire, until it's nearly dead?
It almost ate that poor young maiden Nell;
and just as she was hoping to be wed.

Oh Knave, don't bother me with flippin brips.
For thou should know it works up my poor bloat.
So begone afore my truggles start to jip,
or thou shalt join yon Driggly in yon moat.

The Driggly goes on eating poppin fricks.
While the peasants are still poking it with sticks.

Looking For Santa

The tree is all covered in tinsel,
and the prezzies are piled underneath,
and me Granny's been moaning forever
cos the dog has chewed her false teeth

Me mam is still stuffing the turkey;
there's stuffing all over her sleeve.
But me, I'm looking for Santa
cos at last it's arrived – Christmas Eve!

I've only asked for a train set,
a cricket bat and a new ball.
But me mam says 'Get out of me curtains
or he won't be coming at all'.

Me dad's got the Radio Times;
to see what there is on the box.
He says he don't know what the fuss is
cos all he will get is more socks.

But I'm still looking for Santa,
though I don't think he's coming to me;
cos why would he come down our chimney,
when the prezzies are under the tree?

My Diet Diary

Monday
I'm going to start a diet;
one I haven't tried before.
You just liquidise your cabbage;
then a cabbage drink you pour.

But then I'll need some chocolate.
Just a little piece of chocolate.
And when I've eaten all my chocolate,
I won't buy any more.

Tuesday
My friend gave me a Detox book,
it's wonderful they say.
It's beans with everything – I think.
But the pounds just fall away.'

So when I've finished off my chocolate,
It's such a little piece of chocolate.
A tiny bit of chocolate
makes no difference anyway.

Wednesday
Now today I'm really trying.
I'll have fish for every meal.
Just think of all the weight I'll lose
and how good I'm going to feel.

But I need the taste of chocolate.
I know I've got some chocolate.
Please pass my bar of chocolate;
then an apple I will peel.

Thursday
Today I shall be starting
a diet to make me thin.
But when I come to think of it,
is chocolate such a sin?

So sit and share my chocolate.
You know how you love chocolate.
I'll pop out for more chocolate.
Then this book goes in the bin

Friday

My Birthday Surprise

*My sons have made this challenge,
and so this has to be;
that I write about the present,
that their father gave to me.*

*It was on my birthday morning
when I opened up my eyes,
I saw a gift of large proportions.
And it sure was a surprise.*

*It was wrapped in some old sheeting.
No pretty paper here.
He never could be bothered,
He'd always made that clear.*

*I thought 'it's my old ironing board,
he's bought a cover – new'
You'll find this hard to understand.
That's the sort of thing he'd do!*

*It was a ladder for the loft!!
My tears began to flow.
He's never been romantic,
so this I ought to know.*

Well that day was not a happy one,
he tried to add good news,
'I've also fetched a catalogue,
so a kettle you can choose.'

I suppose he did look sorry,
and later on that night,
to both our sons my husband said
'I never get it right.'

He really looked downhearted,
but quick came their reply;
'So Dad, what kind of ladder,
did mom hope that you would buy'?

Out To Graze

*Well, I've cleared my desk
and my stuff's packed away;
they're putting me out to graze today.
It's a worrying thing, this 'growing old'
All those aches and pains and feeling the cold.*

*The creaking back and the poor old knees.
Then there's the mind – 'old timers disease'
Putting things down and forgetting where,
and hearing folks say – 'well she's not all there.'*

*When the libidos spent – and the sex drives gone,
it's only the telly that gets turned on.
But I'm ok now, no need to fuss.
I've got my pass for the Dudley bus.*

*I've got my glass where my teeth will soak;
but the pension scheme turned out a joke.
My prescriptions are free – so no worries there,
and my leaving gift is a Stannah stair.*

Now, what was I saying? It'll come to me soon;
but I don't want to waste your whole afternoon.
There's someone who'll visit to do my feet.
I can go to the pictures and get a cheap seat.

I might get home help, there's community care.
I can travel by train and get a cheap fare.
On Wednesday I'm booked for my first hair do;
at pensioner's rates, with a blue rinse too.

Phone and tell me the gossip and what's going on.
But remember to shout, 'cos my hearing's gone.
They're putting me out to graze – did I say?
I'd better get going, I really can't stay.

Christmas Day in the Workhouse

When my Granny came through the ceiling,
it was such a strange thing to see.
Her boot, hung among decorations,
was dripping snow all over me.

But that was a minor problem
that my dad had that Christmas Eve.
While they were all down at her house,
what I found you'd never believe.

I'd arrived home late after dancing;
I'd been out with my latest bloke.
I opened the door, never guessing,
that the house was billowing smoke.

Now my dad was a local fireman
and soon the brigade would appear.
Dad's mates all turned up on the engine;
and were grinning from ear to ear.

*So my bed, with electric blanket,
was dragged out for all to see.
It was certainly 'nice and toasty'
like mom always left it for me.*

*The next day kept dad very busy;
re-wiring the house straight away.
All the floorboards had to be lifted,
and so that's how he spent Christmas Day.*

*But that's not the end of the story;
my Gran arrived wanting to see.
That's when she came through the ceiling
and dripped her size fives over me.*

Grandad's Been At The Bottle

Grandad's been dying his hair.

'He's a silly old fool' says my Gran.

He decided to give it some colour

now it's the shade of Orangutan.

Choose Cheese

Spread my scone with Mascapone.
Melt my taste buds with fondue.
I'm fighting fit for Feta
and I'd die for Danish Blue.
Give me Raclette on my baguette.
Slice some pear on Camembert.
Top my Parma ham with Parmisan
and my toast with Gruyere.

I'd like all of these for breakfast
and for lunch and dinner too.
I've a cheesy grin for cheeses,
in fact any cheese will do.
So when I'm feeling peckish,
and can have just what I please,
that's right, my word you've guessed it,
I always say 'Choose Cheese.'

Exercise

A fact that everyone knows;

excercise means touch your toes.

But if this isn't poss.

then I don't give a toss,

if my belly just constantly grows.

The Grass is Always Greener

The grass is at my elbow.
The weeds are to my knees.
I'd like to start the mowing,
But that will make me wheeze.

The pollen starts me coughing.
Hay fever's such a pain.
Just looking at a mower,
will make me sneeze again.

So I'll sit here in my deck chair.
drinking G & T real slow.
'Cos there's nothing I like better,
than to sit and watch grass grow.

Fried or Boiled

Mummy warned you; to be fair.
You promised her that you'd take care.
She said our brother got well oiled;
how he succumbed and then got boiled.
'I'm smart' to all we heard you boast.
'You won't find me on someone's toast'

> *You lied,*
> *you lied!*
> *And now –*
> *You're fried!*

Epitaph

Here lies a Poet
How absurd;
She choked upon
Her final word.

About the Author

Patricia Little is from Walsall in the West Midlands.

She retired some years ago from the MoD where she had worked a cartographer and now resides in Cheshire.

She has been painting for as long as she can remember and has sold her work internationally.

She had her first poem published at the age of ten which was featured in a new comic called The Robin, where she was awarded first prize.

Patricia started to write more prolifically after she retired and has published two children's books.

This is Patricia's first published collection of her poetry.

Sometimes serious; she enjoys writing sonnets in their many forms. Patricia also writes parodies and loves to find the funny side of life; quite a few of her poems are about things that have happened to her, or her family and friends.

On top of the wardrobe,
all covered in dust,
there lies an old suitcase,
full of things that are bust..............